Grandma Jenny's Trip

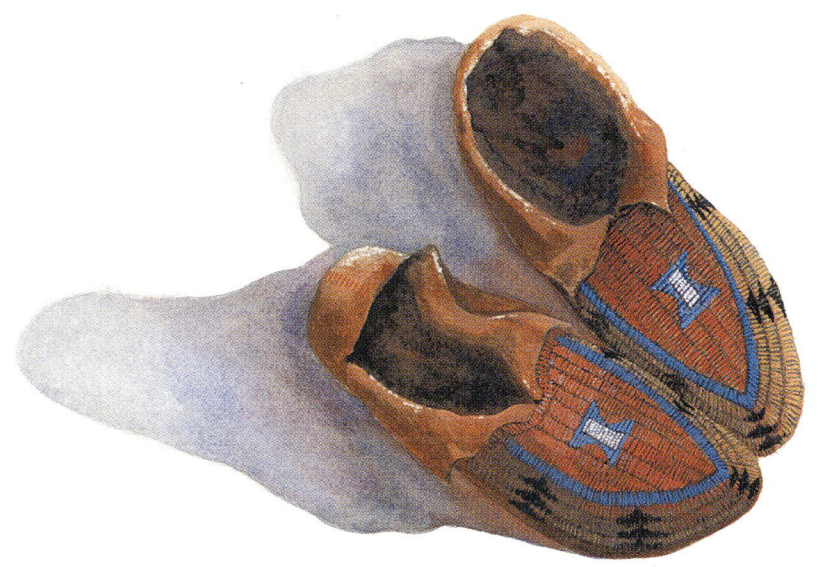

Bently Spang
Illustrated by Ben Carter

Rigby

To the loving memory of all my grandmothers—
you all gave me so much

© 1997 by Rigby,
a division of Reed Elsevier Inc.
1000 Hart Rd.
Barrington, IL 60010-2627

All rights reserved. No part of this publication may be reproduced or transmitted in any form or by any means, electronic or mechanical, including photocopying, recording, taping, or any information storage and retrieval system, without permission in writing from the publisher.

04 03
10 9 8 7 6

Printed in Singapore

ISBN 0-7635-3144-8

Grandma Jenny's kitchen echoed with the shouts of her grandchildren. They all wanted the same thing. "Tell us a story, Grandma Jenny! Please, Grandma!" they pleaded.

Grandma Jenny Spang sat at her kitchen table in Lame Deer, Montana. She was slicing deer meat into thin sheets for drying. Grandpa Wilfred was helping her.

"All right, grandchildren," she said, "I'll tell you a story. This story is a *true* story. It's about a special trip my family took every summer when I was your age.

"It was a trip that took us from our home here on the Northern Cheyenne reservation to Miles City, Montana, 100 miles away. It was a real adventure because we traveled the whole way on horseback and in a buckboard wagon. We didn't have cars like you do today, so the trip took a lot longer.

"The trip took two weeks. For me, the time flew by. Every day we rode through beautiful painted hills, and we camped out every night. There was always something new and interesting to do. I learned much about Cheyenne culture along the way.

"We made the trip to sell and trade things for supplies for the winter. All year we had been tanning hides, beading moccasins and jewelry, and preparing food to take with us. Then one day my dad would say, 'Let's go. It's time for the trip!' We would spend a whole day loading the wagon with tents, food, and trading goods.

"We must have been quite a sight when we left the next morning. My mom drove the overflowing wagon. My sisters and I were so excited that we scampered from one end of the wagon to the other. My dad and my brothers rode horseback. There always seemed to be at least two or three colts following us. The colts ran and kicked as they chased each other.

"The first night's camp was always the most fun. While the rest of us set up camp, Mom cooked a delicious dinner. The smells of dried deer meat, wild turnip, potato, and salt pork in our stew and of freshly made bread were heavenly. The food tasted even better than it smelled. Our meals always tasted better when they were cooked outdoors.

"After dinner the mosquitoes came out. The other children and I made a smudge pot to keep them away. We dug a small hole and built a fire in it. Then we picked fresh sage boughs and put them on the fire. They made a lot of smoke! We danced around the pot and jumped over it. We were pretending we were dancing at a powwow.

"Later that night, Mom and Dad told stories around the campfire. Some were traditional Cheyenne stories about the beginning of the world. Other stories were about when my parents were little and lived the old way. Some were happy stories, but others were sad. The saddest ones were about Cheyenne who had died while fighting the United States cavalry and other American Indians.

"I learned many things from these stories. Every night I fell asleep with my head full of pictures from them.

"One of my favorite things to do during the trip was picking berries. We picked Juneberries, buffaloberries, and chokecherries. I loved to eat ripe chokecherries because they turned my teeth black. Later Mom made them into delicious chokecherry syrup to put on our bread.

"We saw unripe plums and looked forward to picking the ripe fruit on the way home. Plums were fun to pick. We would tie blankets under the plum tree to catch the fruit. Then we would all shake the tree as hard as we could. Plums would fly everywhere! Fortunately most of them would land in the blanket.

"On every trip we stopped at the homes of White ranchers that we knew. If they were butchering cows, we helped them. Afterward they gave us some of the meat and the cows' organs. My mom knew many ways to cook the organs. They were delicious!

"My mom cut the rest of the meat into very thin sheets. Then she used willow sticks to stretch the sheets out and hang them to dry. She said that Cheyenne used to do this to buffalo meat before most of the buffalo were killed. The dried meat didn't spoil for months. We still do this today!

"When we were about an hour away from town, we stopped at the river. There we washed up and put on our best clothes. I put on my best gingham dress and braided my hair tightly. All my family looked so nice. I was very proud as we got ready to ride into camp.

"I loved making the trip, but getting to town was also exciting. You see, many American Indians made this same trip. There were always people from several Indian nations camped at the edge of town. The Northern Cheyenne camp was full of relatives and friends.

"Entering camp was so exciting! Dogs barked and children shouted alongside the wagon. Cries of hello and welcome came from every corner of the camp. I smelled delicious food cooking and heard drums and singing. The whole camp seemed to be moving at once.

"I always felt happy in camp surrounded by so many relatives and other Cheyenne. I realized how important community is to American Indians. There would be many days and nights of delicious meals, stories, and learning from my elders. I also looked forward to the trip home. These times made me realize how fortunate I was to be Cheyenne."